NERDING OUT ABOUT
SCIENCE FICTION

NC

NERD
CULTURE

VIRGINIA LOH-HAGAN

NERD
APPROVED
45TH ‖ PARALLEL
45°

45TH PARALLEL PRESS

Published in the United States of America by Cherry Lake Publishing Group
Ann Arbor, Michigan
www.cherrylakepublishing.com

Reading Adviser: Beth Walker Gambro, MS, Ed., Reading Consultant, Yorkville, IL
Book Designer: Joseph Hatch

Photo Credits: © Supamotion, Adobe Stock, cover, title page; © Kiselev Andrey Valerevich/Shutterstock, 4; Frank R. Paul, Public domain, via Wikimedia Commons, 7; © Jeff Whyte/Shutterstock, 8; © Darryl Brooks/ Shutterstock, 10; Sanna Pudas, CC BY 4.0 via Wikimedia Commons, 12; United States Navy Band from Washington, D.C., USA, Public domain, via Wikimedia Commons, 15; Brett Weinstein, CC BY-SA 2.0 via Wikimedia Commons, 16; © Marko Aliaksandr/Shutterstock, 19; © FrimuFilms/Shutterstock, 21; © Kiselev Andrey Valerevich/Shutterstock, 22; Illustrator T. Allom, Engraver J. Tingle, Public domain, via Wikimedia Commons, 24; © DanieleGay/Shutterstock, 26; © Volha Werasen/Shutterstock, 29

45th Parallel Press is an imprint of Cherry Lake Publishing Group.

Library of Congress Cataloging-in-Publication Data

Names: Loh-Hagan, Virginia, author.
Title: Nerding out about science fiction / by Virginia Loh-Hagan.
Description: Ann Arbor, Michigan : 45th Parallel Press, 2024.
  | Series: Nerd culture | Includes index.
Identifiers: LCCN 2023035094 | ISBN 9781668939376 (paperback)
  | ISBN 9781668938331 (hardcover) | ISBN 9781668940716 (ebook)
  | ISBN 9781668942062 (pdf)
Subjects: LCSH: Science fiction--History and criticism--Juvenile literature.
  | Science fiction films--History and criticism--Juvenile literature.
  | Science fiction television programs--History and criticism--Juvenile literature.
Classification: LCC PN3433.5 .L64 2024 | DDC 809.3/8762--dc23/eng/20230808
LC record available at https://lccn.loc.gov/2023035094

Cherry Lake Publishing Group would like to acknowledge the work of the Partnership for 21st Century Learning, a Network of Battelle for Kids. Please visit Battelle for Kids online for more information.

Note from publisher: Websites change regularly, and their future contents are outside of our control. Supervise children when conducting any recommended online searches for extended learning opportunities.

Printed in the United States of America

Dr. Virginia Loh-Hagan is an author and educator. She is currently the Director of the Asian Pacific Islander Desi American (APIDA) Center at San Diego State University and the Co-Executive Director of The Asian American Education Project. She lives in San Diego with her very tall husband and very naughty dogs.

TABLE OF CONTENTS

Nerds are now trendy. Many nerds play hero roles in movies today.

LIVING THE NERDY LIFE

It's finally cool to be a nerd. Nerd culture is everywhere. It's in movies. It's on TV. It's in video games. It's in books. Everyone is talking about it. Everyone is watching it. Everyone is doing it. There's no escaping nerd culture.

Nerds and sports fans are alike. They have a lot in common. Instead of sports, nerds like nerdy things. Magic is nerdy. Science fiction is nerdy. Superheroes are nerdy. Nerds obsess over these interests. They're huge fans. They have a great love for a topic. They learn all they can. They spend hours on their hobbies. Hobbies are activities. Nerds hang with others who feel the same.

Nerds form **fandoms**. Fandoms are nerd networks. They're communities of fans. Nerds host online group chats. They host meetings. They host **conventions**. Conventions are large gatherings. They have speakers. They have workshops. They're also called **expos**. Tickets sell fast. Everyone wants to go. Nerd conventions are the place to be.

Nerd culture is on the rise. It's very popular. But it didn't used to be. Nerds used to be bullied. They were made fun of. They weren't seen as cool. They'd rather study than party. This made them seem odd. They were seen as different. Not anymore! Today, nerds rule!

15¢

DYNAMIC
SCIENCE STORIES

LORD OF TRANERICA
complete novel by
STANTON COBLENTZ

FEB.

MUTINEERS OF SPACE
novelet by
LLOYD ESHBACK

*PLUS OTHER
GREAT
STORIES*

A RED CIRCLE MAGAZINE

Magazines are another way for nerds to connect. Many fans make their own!

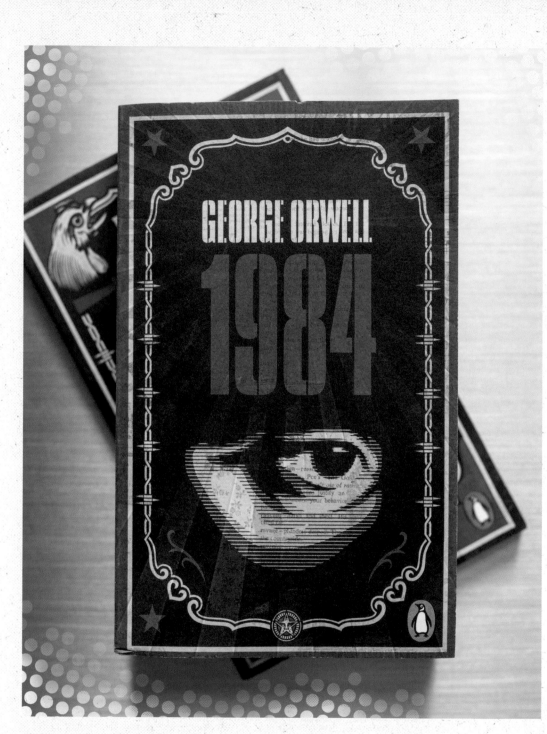

There is soft sci-fi. It addresses human rights issues.

CHAPTER 1

MIXING SCIENCE AND IMAGINATION

Science fiction is also called **sci-fi**. It's a **genre** of fiction. Genre means type. Sci-fi is popular in books. It's popular in movies. It's popular on TV.

Sci-fi is an imagined future. It's about an imagined world. It can be about space. It can be about aliens. It can be about time travel. It can be about robots. It can be about different worlds.

It's based on science. But it's not limited by science. It goes beyond what we know now. It explores what could be true. Hard sci-fi is based on STEM. STEM is science, technology, engineering, and math. It's based on proven facts. Soft sci-fi is based on history and politics. It's based on ideas.

Sci-fi fans love conventions. They meet in person. Dragon Con is one big U.S. convention. Comic-Con is another.

Sci-fi lovers were the first big fandom. They organized into groups. They formed clubs. They hosted conventions. They created demand for sci-fi. They made sci-fi popular.

Sci-fi fans are not limited by sci-fi. They also formed "**fringe** fandoms." Fringe means outside of the main group. Some sci-fi fans break into other groups. They join comic book fandoms. They join gaming fandoms. They join **fantasy** fandoms. Fantasy is a genre. It's based on magic. It's based on myths. Sci-fi and fantasy get mixed up. But they're different.

Most sci-fi fans have a focus. They focus on a writer. They focus on a story. They focus on specific ideas.

There is a top sci-fi award. It is named after Hugo Gernsback. It's called the Hugo Award.

CHAPTER 2

FROM MAGAZINES TO MOVIES

Science fiction became a popular term in the 1920s. Sci-fi fandoms started with American magazines. It grew into books. Then it boomed with TV and movies. TV and movies brought sci-fi into the mainstream.

Hugo Gernsback (1884–1967) was an editor. He published the first sci-fi magazine. The magazine was called *Amazing Stories*. Fans wrote letters. Their addresses were printed. Fans wrote to each other. They debated ideas. They shared their love of sci-fi. They formed local fan clubs. They hosted conventions. The first sci-fi convention was in 1937. It was in Philadelphia.

Sci-fi fans created **fanzines**. They were the first to do so. This started in the 1930s. Fanzines are homemade magazines.

NERD LINGO!

FIRST CONTACT
This term is used in space stories. It's when humans and aliens first meet.

FOURTH DIMENSION
Things take up space. There are 3 dimensions of space. They are length, width, and height. Some think there are more. Sci-fi fans believe in a fourth dimension. The fourth dimension is time.

SLAN SHACK
Some sci-fi fans live together. Their home is called a slan shack. Slan refers to sci-fi fans. "Fans are slans" is a popular saying. It means sci-fi fans are smart. It means they are smarter than others. It explains why they're made fun of. It comes from a book. The book is called *Slan*. It is by A. E. van Vogt. Slan is a race of evolved humans. They're targeted for being smarter.

TECHNOBABBLE
Technobabble means nonsense words. Characters in sci-fi may use such words. They're used to explain unlikely events. These words sound fancy. They sound important. But they're made up. They're not real.

Sci-fi **pulp** magazines emerged. Pulp is cheap wood paper. These magazines were made quickly. The stories were easy to read. They were fun. Fans loved them. They read them every month. Today, sci-fi fans write and read stories online.

Sci-fi fans become sci-fi creators. Many sci-fi writers started as fans. Jules Verne (1828–1905) was an early sci-fi writer. So was H. G. Wells (1866–1946). Mary Shelley (1797–1851) wrote *Frankenstein*. Many think this was the first sci-fi book. Their books were hits. Young readers read their books. They fell in love with sci-fi. They became creators themselves. Fans make sci-fi TV and movies. They create more fans.

Over time, more and more women entered sci-fi fandoms.

Star Trek fans are called Trekkies.

CHAPTER 3

OUT OF THIS WORLD

There are different types of sci-fi. **Space opera** is the most popular. These stories are set in outer space. They're about space travel. They're about aliens. They include space warfare. They have heroes. They have villains.

The biggest space operas are *Star Wars* and *Star Trek*. Both are hugely popular. Both have movies. Both have TV shows. Both feature many planets. Both feature many species. Both have lots of products. Fans buy and collect props.

Star Wars is about a civil war. Rebels and the Empire fight for power. *Star Trek* is about a starship. The crew explores new worlds. Fans love debating which space opera is better.

NERD TO KNOW!

Marc Okrand was born in 1948. He studies languages. He's an expert on Indigenous languages. He's an expert on Southeast Asian native languages. He created the Klingon language. Klingon is used in the *Star Trek* series. The Klingons are a fictional species. They're humanoids. They're warriors. They have ridged foreheads. They're popular characters. They're in all the TV shows and movies. James Doohan (1920–2005) was a *Star Trek* actor. He said nonsense words. Okrand based a language on those words. He wrote books about Klingon. He wrote a dictionary. He wrote a book of sayings. He wrote a cultural guide. He wrote an opera. He himself speaks Klingon. Many fans speak Klingon. Klingon is spoken around the world. It's the most popular fictional language. It has a world record for most speakers. Shakespeare's works have been translated to Klingon. The Bible has been translated to Klingon. Okrand also created other *Star Trek* languages.

Sci-fi fans love stories about aliens. A popular theme is alien invasions. Humans fear aliens. They fear them taking over. They fear them destroying the planet. They fear them eating humans. The most known early alien invasion story is *The War of the Worlds*. H. G. Wells wrote this book. It was first published in parts in 1897.

Some stories feature aliens taking human form. Some feature aliens helping humans. Some feature humans invading alien planets. Some feature humans rebelling against alien masters.

Some people believe in aliens. They think there's life beyond Earth. There's no proof of aliens. But fans imagine there's life beyond Earth.

Some people claim aliens have kidnapped them.

Time travel is a popular theme. *Doctor Who* is a British TV show. Doctor Who is a time lord. They're an alien. They look human. They explore the universe. They time travel via the TARDIS. The TARDIS looks like a blue phone booth. The show is the longest-running sci-fi show.

History doesn't change in time travel. People can go back in time. But they can't change events that have happened. **Alternate** history is different. Alternate means another version. In these stories, history is changed. Alternate history stories present different timelines. An example is *The Man in the High Castle*. It was written by Philip K. Dick. It's about what would happen if the Allies lost World War II (1939–1945).

Doctor Who's time travel machine, the TARDIS. The Inside is much bigger than the outside.

Zombie stories are popular right now.

Dystopian stories are about fear. They imagine destroyed worlds. People lose their freedoms. They suffer a lot. An example is *The Hunger Games*. Suzanne Collins wrote this series of books. The books were later made into movies. *The Hunger Games* is about a nation called Panem. Teens fight each other. They fight in a battle to the death. Fans love the books. They love the movies.

Post-apocalyptic stories are also popular. An apocalypse is a disaster. It's an event that destroys the world. It ends life as we know it. People fight to survive. Many video games feature such themes. Some video games become movies or shows. An example is *The Last of Us*. Humans infected with a virus have become zombies. They are hurting people. A man protects a teen girl. Fans like survival stories.

Many sci-fi stories feature tech. They explore how humans and machines live together. Robots can be helpful. Or they can be harmful.

Some sci-fi fans like **cyberpunk**. Cyberpunk is dystopian. It imagines tech taking over. It features high-tech gadgets. Rich people have tech. Poor people do not. Rebels are **hackers**. Hackers break into computers. They know how to code. They tend to be heroes.

Cyberpunk is about the future. Some sci-fi fans like **steampunk**. Steampunk is set in the past. It's usually set in Victorian England (1837–1901). Or it can be set in the American Wild West era (1865–1900). It features steam-powered machines.

The Industrial Revolution (1760–1840) inspired steampunk. It was a time of change. People used to make goods by hand. They started using machines.

TOO NERDY!

Hoaxes are tricks. They're meant to be funny. Sci-fi fans take hoaxes seriously. Some hoaxes sound real. Hoax stories have been printed. There was a hoax about Nibiru. In 1976, a book called *The 12th Planet* was published. It mentioned a planet called Nibiru. A psychic said a planet would crash into Earth. Rumors spread about the Mayan calendar. The Mayan are an ancient people. They're from Mexico. Their calendar ended in 2012. People thought this date was scary. They thought Earth would be wiped out. They thought Nibiru was going to crash into Earth. Nibiru is 4 times larger than Earth. Many people blogged about this. Blogs are online journals. People connected their blogs to NASA. NASA is the U.S. space agency. This made the blogs seem real. Scientists denied Nibiru. They said Nibiru doesn't exist. No crash happened in 2012. That was the biggest proof.

Alien invasion stories are popular. They show that people fear the unknown.

CHAPTER 4

RELEASE YOUR INNER NERD

You, too, can be a sci-fi nerd! Try one of these activities!

HOST A SCI-FI BOOK CLUB!

The best way to be a sci-fi fan is to read sci-fi. Then find other sci-fi fans. Discuss your thoughts with them. Take turns picking books. Explore different types. It's good to read different topics. Push the limits of what you know. That's the point of sci-fi.

Sci-fi lets us explore big questions. The topics address what's happening in the world. An example is space stories. These stories are not just about space. They're about our fear of the unknown. We want to know what's out there.

MAKE SCI-FI COSPLAY!

Cosplay means costume play. It's performance art. Cosplayers dress as their favorite characters. They wear makeup. They have props. Some buy costumes. Some make their own costumes. Sci-fi fans dress as sci-fi characters. They dress like aliens. They dress like robots. They create a look of the future. They go to sci-fi conventions.

Making your own costumes is fun. It also saves money. Use pictures as a guide. Duct tape is a great tool. Cut out cardboard shapes. Wrap tape around the cardboard. Get creative!

Learn how to do makeup. Watch videos. Learn to change your face. Use face paint. Add features. Have fun!

Sci-fi fans often do cool makeup for conventions. You can try it yourself!

NERDY TIPS!

TIP #1

FANS LIKE TO TALK
ABOUT DETAILS.
THEY'RE EXPERTS.
THEY KNOW THEIR
SUBJECT MATTER.
THEY KNOW THEIR TOPICS.
MAKE SURE TO
STUDY SCIENCE.
READ SCIENCE BOOKS.
READ SCIENCE MAGAZINES.
WATCH SCIENCE SHOWS.
INTERVIEW SCIENTISTS.

TIP #2

BE CURIOUS. ASK QUESTIONS.
ASK YOURSELF, "WHAT IF...?"
WONDER ABOUT EVERYTHING.
IMAGINE WHAT COULD HAPPEN.
SCI-FI COMES FROM EXPLORING IDEAS.
SCI-FI FANS DON'T LIMIT
THEMSELVES TO REALITY.
THEY GO BEYOND THE HERE AND NOW.
THEY PUSH BOUNDARIES.